PIANO • VOCAL • GUITAR

PINK
GREATEST HITS... SO FAR!!!

MW00781884

CONTENTS

ISBN 978-1-61780-638-4

7777 W. BLUEMOUND RD. P.O. BOX 13819 MILWAUKEE, WI 53213

GET THE PARTY STARTED

Words and Music by
LINDA PERRY

* Vocal written one octave higher than sung.

N.C. Bm

Get this party started on a Saturday night. Ev'rybody's waitin' for me to arrive. Sending out the message to all of my friends. We'll be lookin' flashy in my Mercedes Benz. I get lots of style, got my gold diamond rings. I can go for miles if you know what I mean.

volume, breakin' down to the beat. Cruisin' through the west side we'll be checkin' the scene. Boulevard is freakin' as I'm comin' up fast. I'll be burnin' rubber, you'll be kissin' my ass. Pull up to the bumper, get out of the car. License plate says "Stunner Number One Superstar."

nection as I enter the room. Ev'rybody's chillin' as I set up the groove. Pumpin' up the volume with this brand new beat. Ev'rybody's dancin' and they're dancin' for me. I'm your operator, you can call anytime. I'll be your connection to the party line.

To Coda
I'm com - in' up so you
bet - ter get this par - ty start - ed. I'm com - in' up I'm com - in'. I'm
com - in' up so you bet - ter get this par - ty start - ed.
Pump - in' up the
Get this par - ty
start - ed.

Bm9
Bm
Bm9
Bm
D.S. al Coda
N.C.
Mak - in' my con-
CODA
I'm com - in' up so you bet - ter get this par - ty start - ed
Play 3 times
I'm com - in' up,
uh huh.
I'm com - in'.
you bet - ter.
I'm com - in' up so you
bet - ter get this par - ty start - ed.
Get this par - ty start - ed.

Get this party started right now. Get this party
started. Get this party started.
Get this party started right now.
N.C.

THERE YOU GO

Words and Music by ALECIA MOORE,
KANDI L. BURRUSS and KEVIN BRIGGS

* Recorded a half step higher.
** Melody is written an octave higher than sung.

Am
game, so your best bet is to be straight with me. So you
you, 'cause my life was all a - bout you. So you
E7
say you wan - na talk, let's talk. If you won't talk, I'll walk. Yes, like that. I've
say you wan - na talk, I don't. Say you wan - na change, I won't. Yes, like that.
Am
got a new man, he's wait - ing out back, now what? What - cha think a - bout that? Now
Had your chance, won't take you back, now what? What - cha think a - bout that? And
E7
when I say I'm through, I'm through. Ba - sic - 'ly I'm through with you. What - cha wan - na say?

Am
Had to have it your way, had to play games, now you're beg - ging me to stay. There you
E7
go, look - in' pi - ti - ful, just be - cause I let you go. There you
Am
go, talk - in' 'bout you want me back, but some - times it be's like that. So there you
E7
go, talk - in' 'bout you miss me so, that you love me so, why let you go?

1
Am
There you go, 'cause your life's not whole.
Look at you, there you go.
2
Am
Dm7
Look at you, there you go.
Don't you wish you could turn the hands of time,
Am
E7
don't you wish that you still were mine,
don't you wish I'd take you back, don't you
Am
G
Fmaj7
Em
Dm7
wish that things were sim-ple like that? Oh,
did-n't miss a good thing 'til it's gone,

Am
E7
but I knew it wouldn't be long 'til you came run-ning back,
Am
mis-sing my love. There you go.
There you go, look-in' pi-ti-ful
E7
just be-cause I let you go. There you go, talk-in' 'bout you want me back, but
Am
some-times it be's like that. There you go, talk-in' 'bout you miss me so, that you

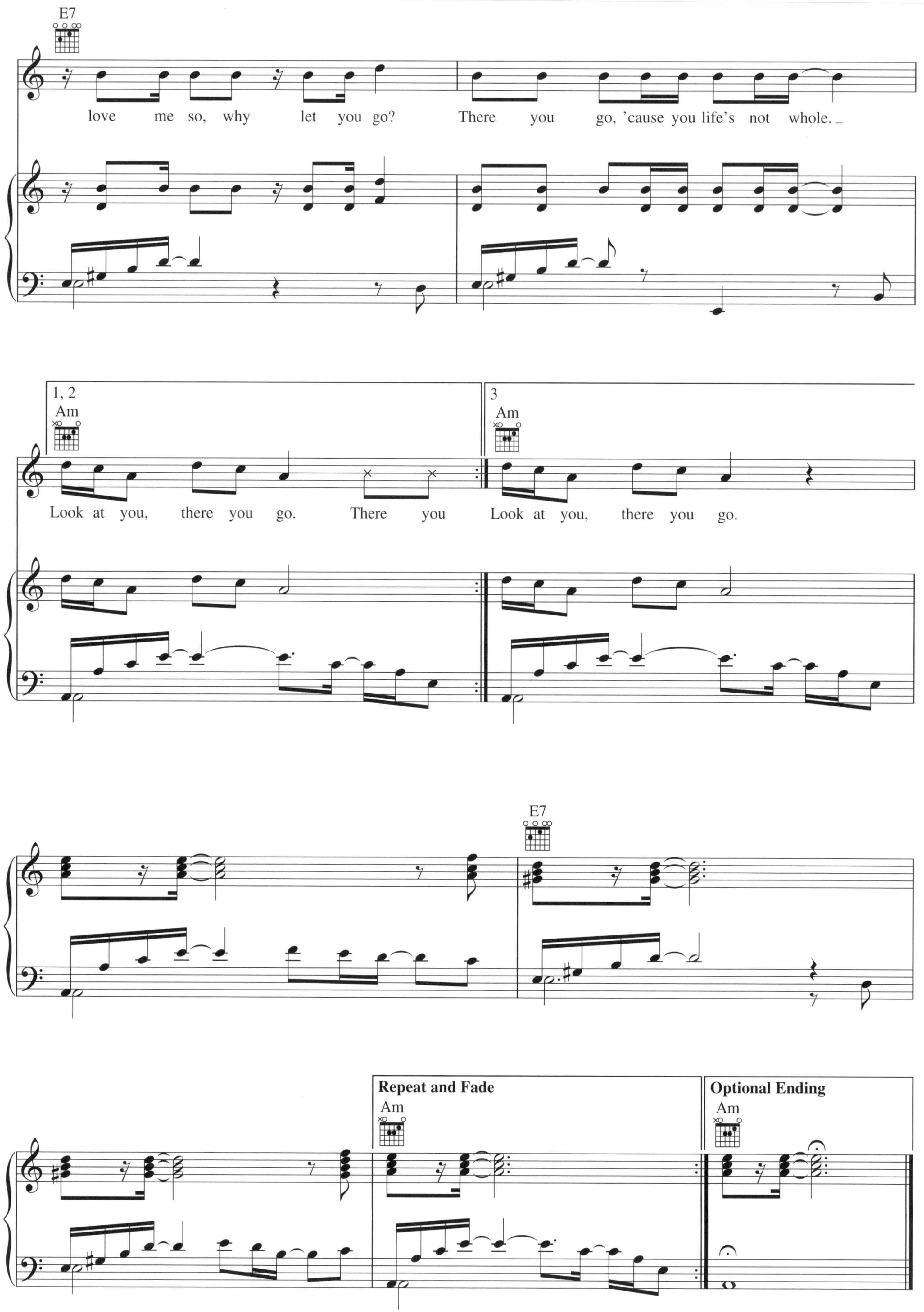
E7
love me so, why let you go? There you go, 'cause you life's not whole. _
1, 2
Am
Look at you, there you go. There you
3
Am
Look at you, there you go.
E7
Repeat and Fade
Am
Optional Ending
Am

DON'T LET ME GET ME

Words and Music by ALECIA MOORE
and DALLAS AUSTIN

B♭
Ev - 'ry - day I fight a war a - gainst the mir - ror,
So doc - tor, doc - tor, won't you please pre - scribe me some - thing.
A♭
4fr
B♭
I can't take the per - son star - ing back at me.
A day in the life of some - one else.
I'm a haz - ard to my -
E♭
3fr
Cm
3fr
B♭
- self.
Don't let me get me,
I'm my own worst en - e - my.
A♭
4fr
E♭
3fr
Cm
3fr
It's bad when you an - noy your - self,
so ir - ri - tat - ing.

B♭
A♭
4fr
Don't wan - na be my friend no more,
I wan - na be some - bod - y else.
1
E♭
3fr
Cm
3fr
B♭
I wan - na be some - bod - y else.
A♭
4fr
2
E♭
3fr
Cm
3fr
Don't let me get me,
B♭
A♭
4fr
I'm my own worst en - e - my.
It's bad when you an - noy your -

E♭
3fr
Cm
3fr
- self,
so ir - ri - tat - ing.
B♭
A♭
4fr
Don't wan - na be my friend no more,
I wan - na be some - bod - y else.
B♭
Doc - tor, doc - tor, won't you please pre - scribe me some - thing,
A♭
4fr
B♭
D.S. al Coda
a day in the life of some - one else. Don't let me get me.

CODA
A♭
4fr
E♭
3fr
Solo ends I'm a haz-ard to my - self,
Cm
3fr
B♭
A♭
4fr
Don't let me get me, I'm my own worst en - e - my. It's bad when you an - noy your -
E♭
3fr
Cm
3fr
B♭
- self, so ir - ri - tat - ing. Don't wan - na be my friend no more,
A♭
4fr
Repeat and Fade
E♭
3fr
Optional Ending
E♭
3fr
I wan-na be some - bod - y else.

JUST LIKE A PILL

E5
D5
5fr
E5
— sup - port, there's a short-age in the switch. — I can't stay on your mor - phine, 'cause it's mak-ing me itch. —
3
D5
5fr
E5
— I said I tried to call — the nurse — a - gain, but she's being a lit - tle bitch. —
D5
5fr
E5
To Coda
A5
5fr
— I think I'll get out — of here, where I can run just as fast as I can —
F♯5
D5
5fr
E5
— to the mid - dle of no - where, — to the mid - dle of my frus - trat - ed fears. — And I

A5
F♯5
D5
swear, you're just like a pill. 'Stead of mak-ing me bet - ter, you keep mak-ing me ill,
E5
A5
F♯5
you keep mak-ing me ill. Run just as fast as I can to the mid-dle of no - where,
D5
E5
A5
to the mid-dle of my frus - trat - ed fears. And I swear, you're just like a pill.
F♯5
D5
E5
D.S. al Coda
'Stead of mak-ing me bet - ter, you keep mak-ing me ill, you keep mak-ing me ill.

CODA
A5
F♯5
run just as fast as I can to the mid-dle of no-where,
D5
E5
to the mid-dle of my frus-trat-ed fears. And I
A5
F♯m
D5
swear, you're just like a pill. 'Stead of mak-ing me bet-ter, you keep mak-ing me ill,
Repeat and Fade
E5
you keep mak-ing me
Optional Ending
E5
A5
you keep mak-ing me ill.

FAMILY PORTRAIT

Words and Music by ALECIA MOORE
and SCOTT STORCH

E♭
3fr
Dm
G
I told God you did-n't mean those nas-ty things you said.
I know that she hurts you, but re-mem-ber, I love you too.
Cm
3fr
Fm
You fight a-bout mon-ey, 'bout me and my broth-er,
I ran a-way to-day, ran from the noise, ran a-way.
E♭
3fr
Dm
G
3
and this I come home to, this is my shel-ter.
Don't wan-na go back to that place, but don't have no choice, no way.
Cm
3fr
Fm
It ain't eas-y grow-ing up in World War Three, nev-er know-ing what love could be.
You'll
But I've

E♭
3fr
Dm
G
see, I don't want love to de - stroy me like it has done my fam - i - ly. Can we
seen, did
Cm
Fm
work it out, can we be a fam - i - ly? I prom - ise, I'll be
E♭
Dm
G
bet - ter, Mom - my, I'll do an - y - thing. Can we
Cm
Fm
work it out, can we be a fam - i - ly? I prom - ise, I'll be

E♭
3fr
Dm
G
Cm
3fr
better, Daddy, please don't leave.
In our fam-'ly portrait
Fm
E♭
3fr
we look pretty happy.
Let's play pretend, let's act like it comes
Dm
G
Cm
3fr
nat-'rally.
I don't wanna have to split the holidays,
I don't want
Fm
E♭
3fr
two addresses,
I don't want a stepbrother anyway,
and I don't want my

Dm G Cm Fm
mom to have to change her last name. In our fam - 'ly por - trait we look pret - ty hap - py, we look
Eb Dm G Cm
pret - ty nor - mal, let's go back to that. In our fam - 'ly por - trait we look
Fm Eb Dm G
pret - ty hap - py, let's play pre - tend, act like it comes nat - 'ral - ly. In our
Can we
Cm Fm
fam - 'ly por - trait we look pret - ty hap - py, we look
work it out, can we be a fam - i - ly? I prom - ise I'll be

E♭
3fr
Dm
G
pret - ty nor - mal, let's go back to that. In our
bet - ter, Mom - my, I'll do an - y - thing. Can we
Cm
3fr
1
Fm
fam - 'ly por - trait we look pret - ty hap - py.
work it out, can we be a fam - i - ly? I prom - ise, I'll be
E♭
3fr
Dm
G
3
Let's play pre - tend, act like it comes so nat - 'ral - ly. In our
bet - ter, Dad - dy, please don't leave. Can we
3

2
Fm
E♭
3fr
Dm
G
pret - ty hap - py, we look pret - ty nor - mal, let's go back to that.
fam - i - ly? I prom - ise I'll be bet - ter, Dad - dy, please don't leave.
Cm
3fr
Fm
Dad - dy, don't leave, Dad - dy, don't leave,
E♭
3fr
Dm
G
Dad - dy, don't leave, Dad - dy, don't leave, Dad - dy, don't leave, turn a - round, please.

Cm Fm E♭

Re - mem - ber that the night you left you took my shin - ing

Dm G Cm Fm

star. Dad - dy, don't leave, Dad - dy, don't leave, Dad - dy, don't

E♭ Dm G

leave, don't leave us here a - lone. Ma - ma'll be

Cm Fm E♭

nic - er, I'll be so much bet - ter, I'll tell my broth - er. I won't

Dm G Cm
spill the milk at din - ner. I'll be so much bet - ter, I'll do ev -
Fm Eb
- 'ry - thing right, I'll be your lit - tle girl for - ev - er,
Dm G Cm Fm
I'll go to sleep at night. Oh, oh, oh.
Eb Dm G
Repeat and Fade
(Vocal ad lib.)
Optional Ending
Cm

TROUBLE

Words and Music by ALECIA B. MOORE
and TIM ARMSTRONG

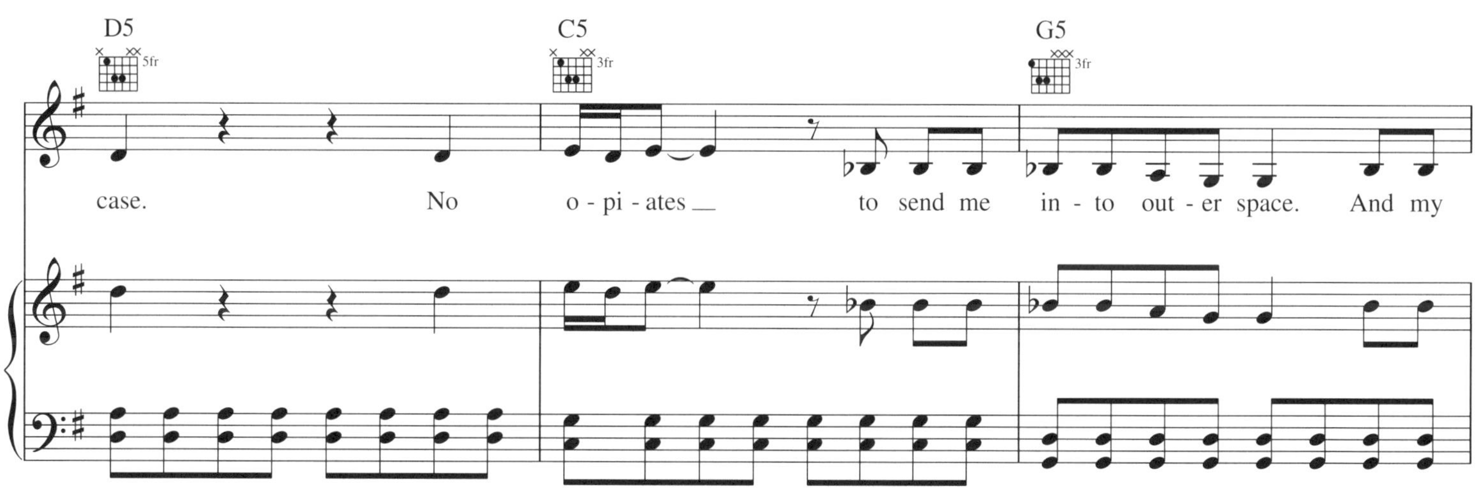

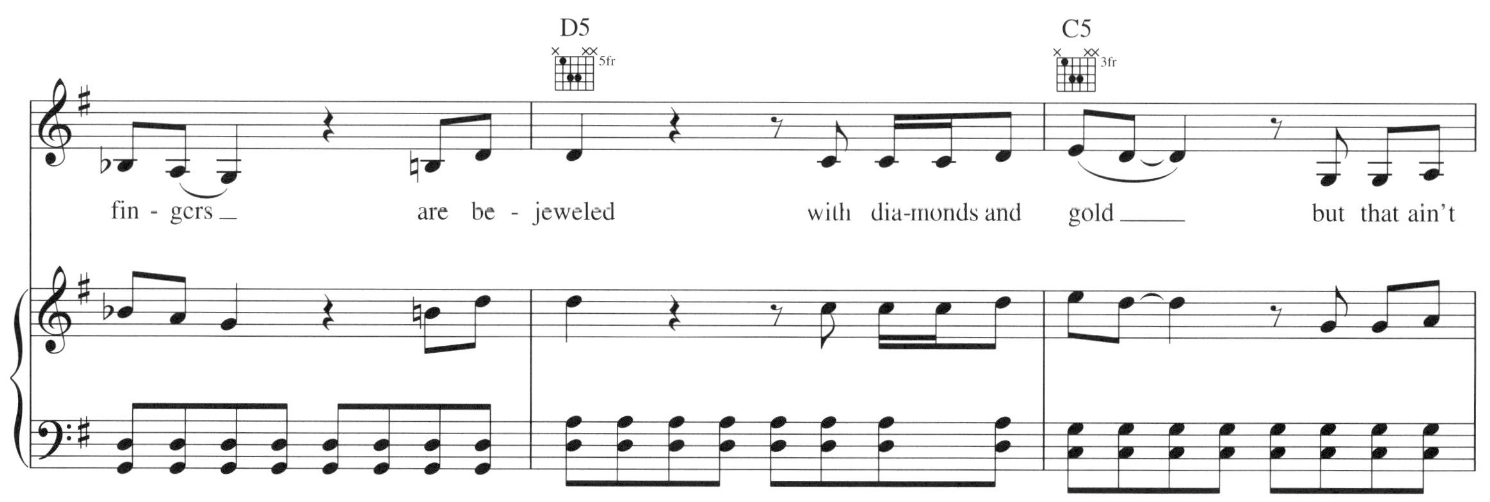

G5 D5 G5 C5 G5 C5
3fr 5fr 3fr 3fr 3fr 3fr
gon - na help me now. I'm trou - ble, yeah, trou - ble now. I'm
G5 C5 D5 C5 G5 C5
3fr 3fr 5fr 3fr 3fr 3fr
trou - ble ya'll. I dis - turb my town. I'm trou - ble, yeah,
G5 C5 G5 C5 D5 C5
3fr 3fr 3fr 3fr 5fr 3fr
trou - ble now. I'm trou - ble ya'll. I got trou - ble in my town. You think you're
G5 D5 C5
3fr 5fr 3fr
right but you were wrong. You tried to take me but I knew

G5
D5
3fr
5fr
all a - long. You can't take me for a ride.
I'm not a
You're not a
C5
G5
D5
G5
C5
fool now so you bet - ter run and hide.
fool now so you bet - ter run and hide.
I'm trou - ble, yeah,
G5
C5
G5
C5
D5
C5
trou - ble now. I'm trou - ble ya'll.
I got trou - ble in my town.
I dis - turb my town.
I'm
G5
C5
G5
C5
G5
C5
trou - ble, yeah, trou - ble now. I'm trou - ble ya'll. I got trou -

D5
C5
5fr
3fr
Bm7
Em7
- ble in my town. If you see me com - ing
Am
C
D
Bm7
down the street then you know it's
To Coda
E7
Am
C
D
time to go. Yeah, you know it's time to go 'cause you got
G5
C5
3fr
trou - ble.

D5 C5 G5 C5 G5 C5
5fr 3fr 3fr 3fr 3fr 3fr
G5 C5 D5 C5
3fr 3fr 5fr 3fr
N.C.
No at - tor - neys to plead my
C5 G5
3fr 3fr
case. No o - pi - ates to send me in - to out - er space. And my
D5 C5
5fr 3fr
fin - gers _ are be - jeweled with dia - monds and gold _ but that ain't

G5
3fr
D.S. al Coda
gon - na help me now. You think you're
CODA
Am
C
D
go, go.
I got
G5
C5
trou - ble,
yeah,
trou - ble now.
I'm
trou - ble ya'll.
I got trou -
D5
5fr
- ble in my town.
I got
trou - ble,
yeah,
trou - ble now.
I'm
trou - ble ya'll.
I got trou
- ble in my town.
I got
trou - ble,
yeah,

G5 C5 G5 C5 D5 C5
3fr 3fr 3fr 3fr 5fr 3fr
trou - ble now. I'm trou - ble ya'll. I got trou - ble in my town. I'm
G5 C5 G5 C5 G5 C5
trou - ble, yeah, trou - ble now. I'm trou - ble ya'll. I got trou -
D5 C5 G5 C5 G5 C5
- ble in my town, yeah, yeah.
G5 C5 D5 C5 G5
I got trou - ble in my town, yeah, yeah.

STUPID GIRLS

Words and Music by ALECIA MOORE,
BILLY MANN, NIKLAS OLOVSON
and ROBIN LYNCH

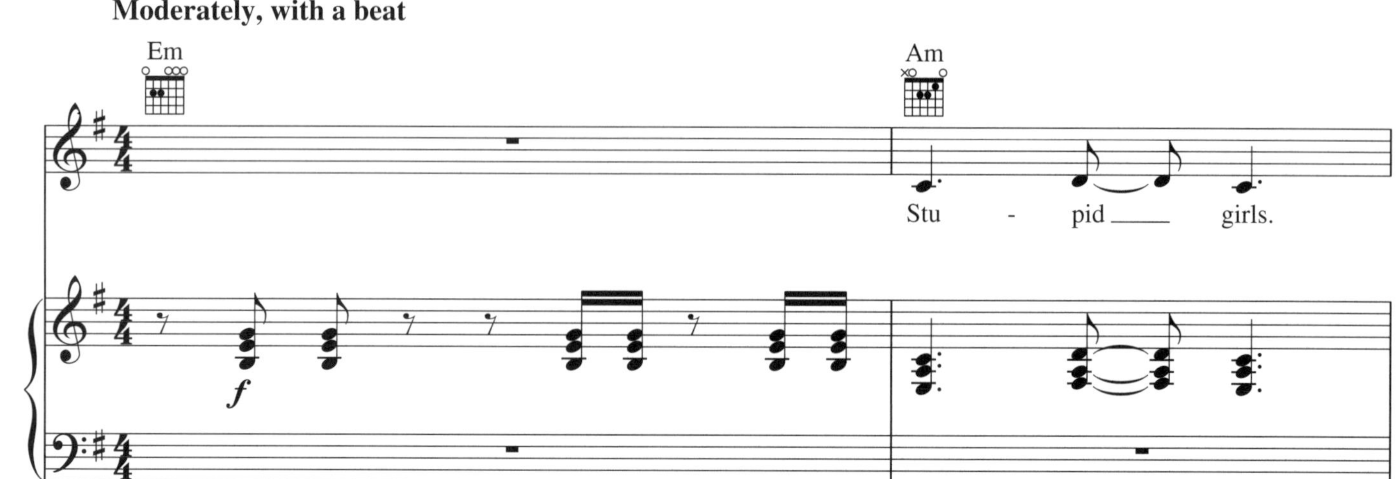

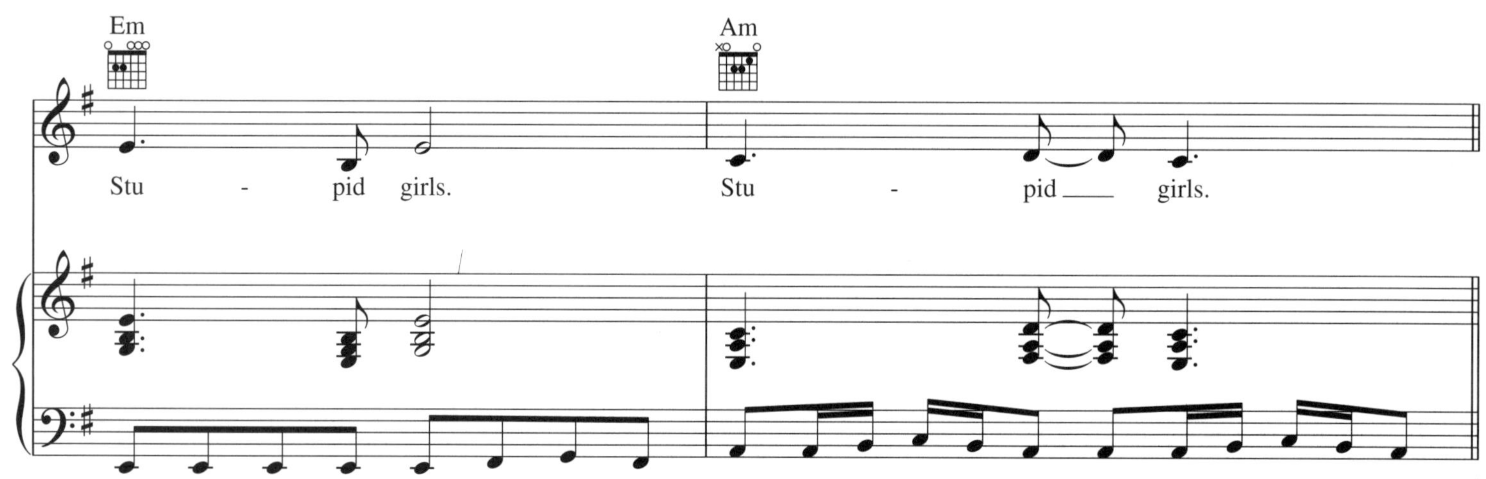

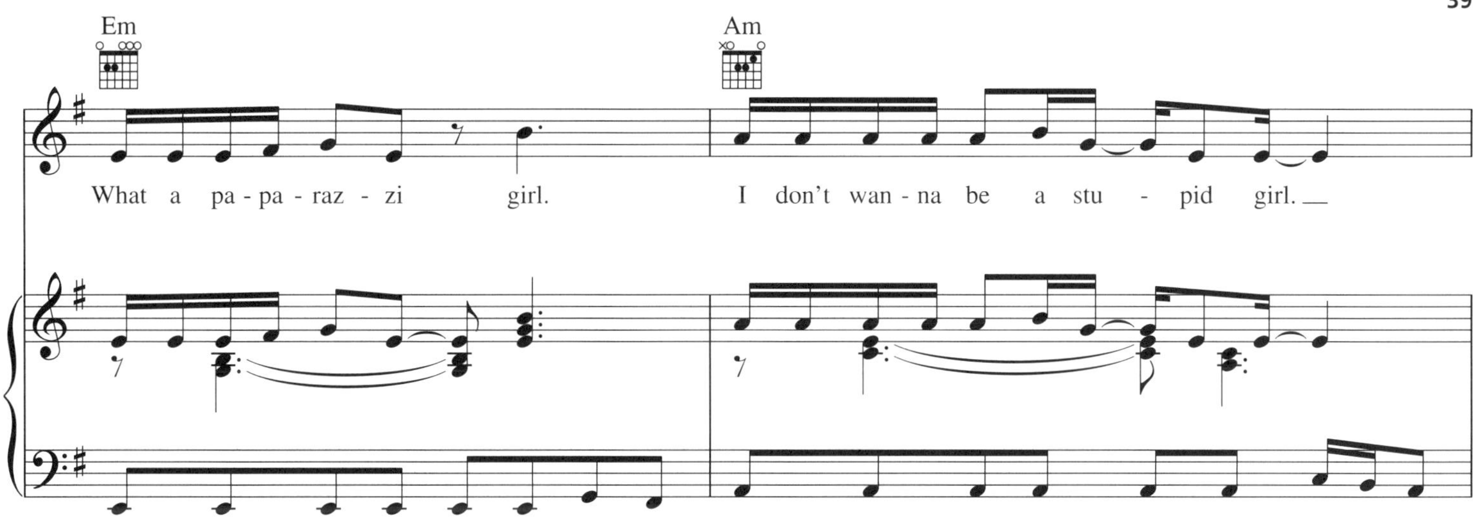
Em
Am
What a pa-pa-raz-zi girl.
I don't wan-na be a stu - pid girl.

Em
Am
Go to Fred Se-gal, you'll find 'em there.
Laugh-in' loud so all the lit-tle peo-ple stare.

Em
Am
Look-in' for a dad-dy to pay for the cham-pagne.
Drop a name. What

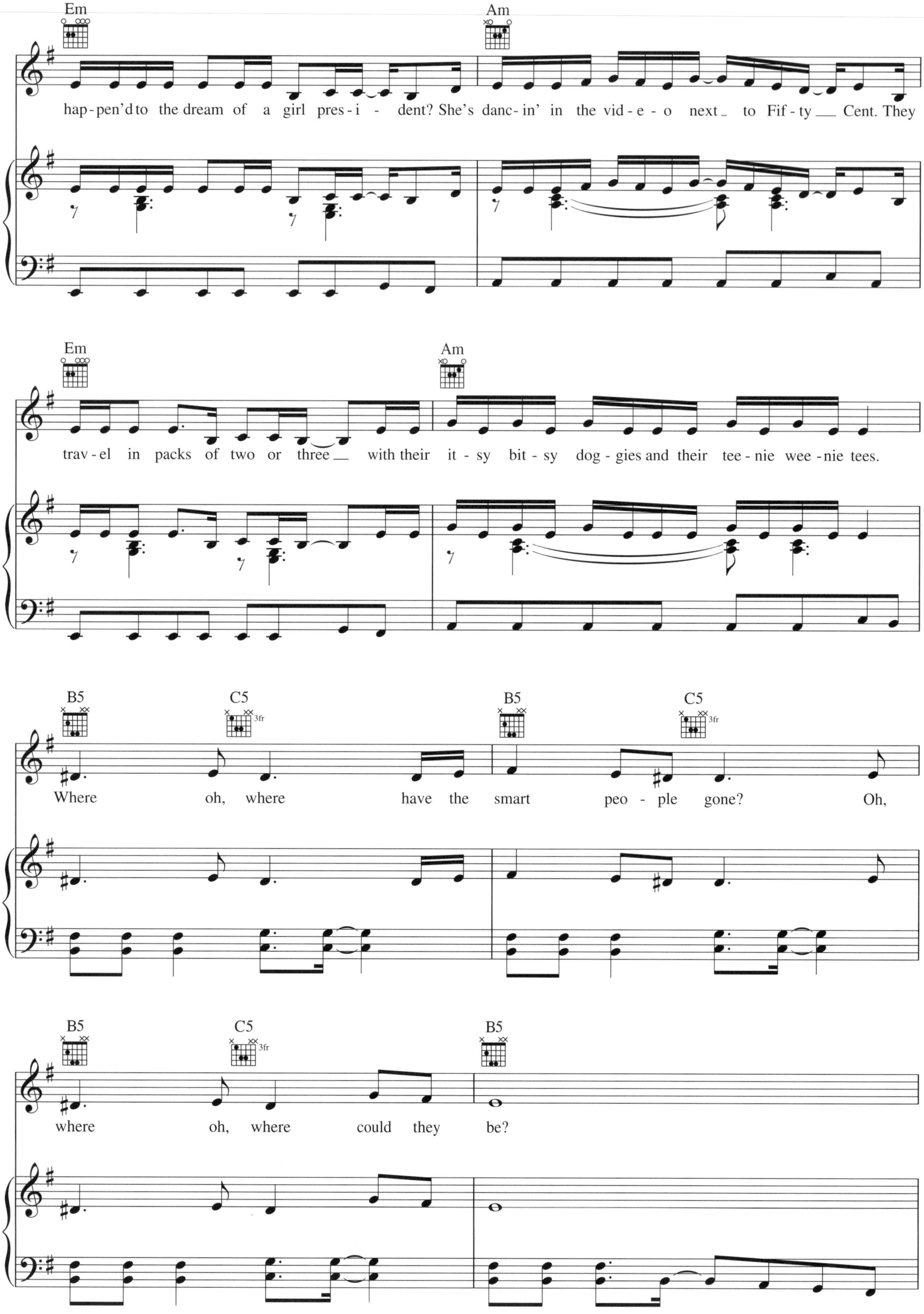
Em
Am
hap-pen'd to the dream of a girl pres-i - dent? She's danc-in' in the vid-e-o next to Fif-ty Cent. They
Em
Am
trav-el in packs of two or three with their it - sy bit - sy dog - gies and their tee - nie wee - nie tees.
B5
C5
3fr
B5
C5
3fr
Where oh, where have the smart peo - ple gone? Oh,
B5
C5
3fr
B5
where oh, where could they be?

Em
Am
Ba - by, if I act like that,
that guy will call me back.
Em
Am
What a pa - pa - raz - zi girl.
I don't wan - na be a stu - pid girl.
Em
Am
Ba - by, if I act like that,
flip - pin' my blond hair back.
Em
Am
To Coda
Push up my bra like that.
I don't wan - na be a stu - pid girl.

E♭m
6fr
Cm
3fr
Am
F♯m
Em
The dis - ease is grow-ing. It's ep - i - dem - ic.
Am
Em
I'm scared that there ain't a cure. The world be-lieves it and I'm go - in' cra - zy.
Am
N.C.
Em
I can - not take an - y - more. I'm so glad that I'll nev - er fit in.
Am
Em
That will nev - er be me. Out - casts and girls with am - bi - tion,

Am
B5
C5
3fr
that's what I wan - na see.
Dis - as - ters all a - round.
A world of de - spair.
Their on - ly con - cern,
N.C.
D.S. al Coda
CODA
Em
will they fuck up my hair?
Pink, and do your thing. Do your
thing and do your thing. Do your huh.
I like this

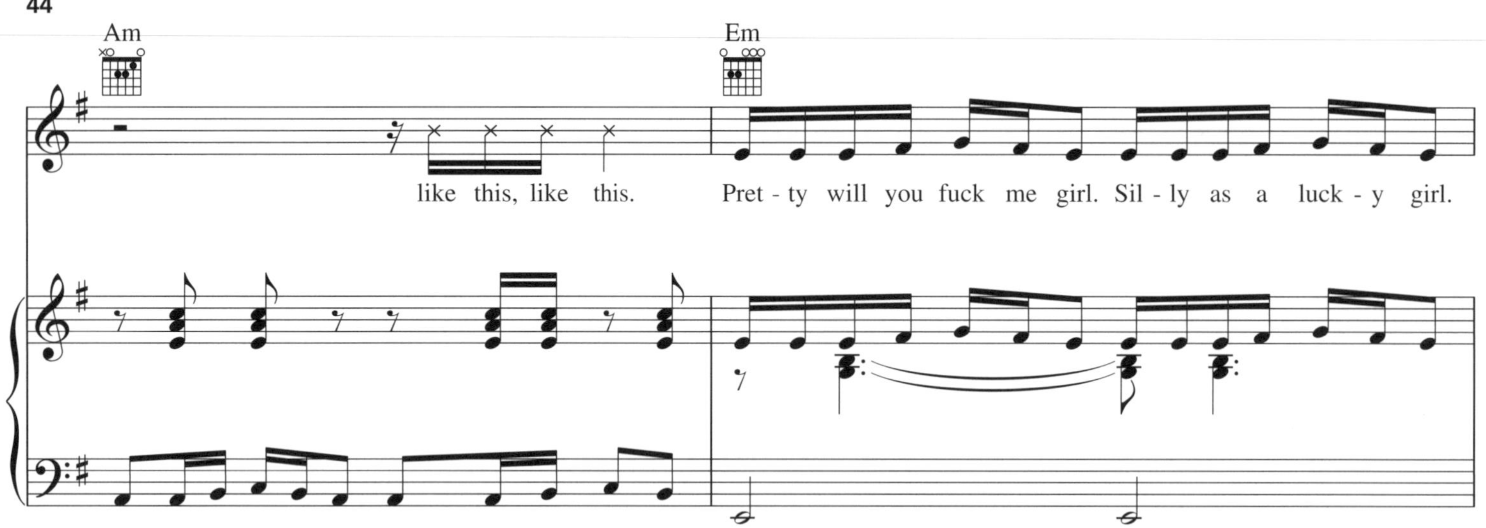
Am
Em
like this, like this.
Pret - ty will you fuck me girl. Sil - ly as a luck - y girl.

Am
Em
Pull my hair, I'll suck it girl. Stu - pid girls.
Pret - ty will you fuck me girl. Sil - ly as a luck - y girl.

N.C.
Em
Pull my hair, I'll suck it girl. Stu - pid girls.
Ba - by, if I, ba - by, if I act like that,

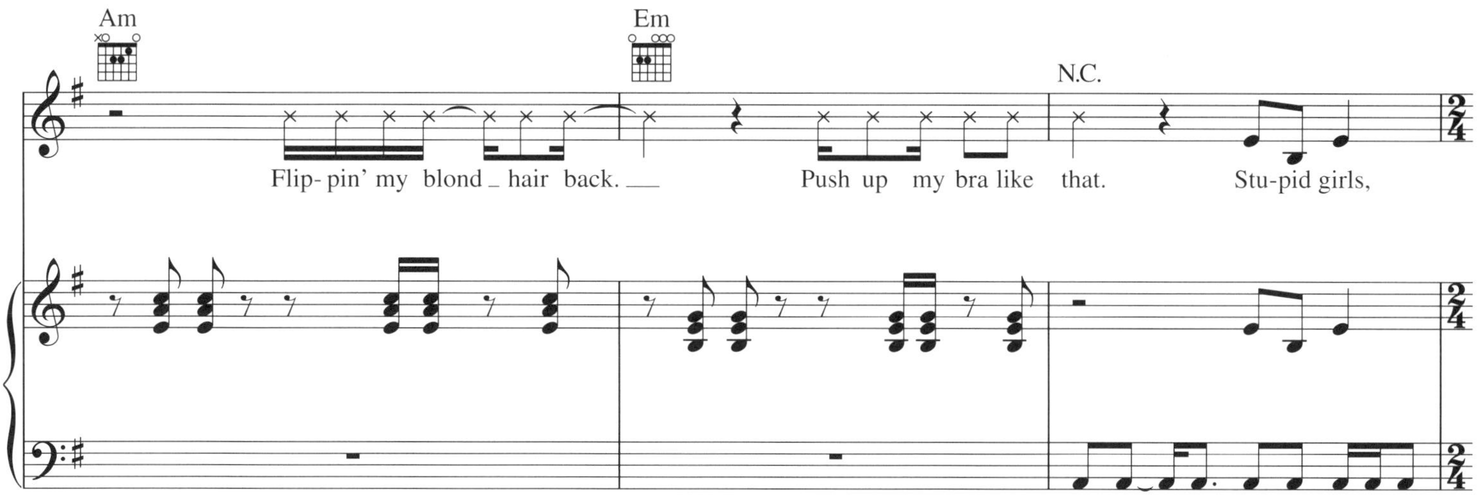
Am
Em
N.C.
Flip- pin' my blond _ hair back. ___
Push up my bra like that.
Stu-pid girls,

Em
Am
girls, girls.
Ba - by, if I act like that,
that guy will call me back.

Em
Am
What a pa - pa - raz - zi girl.
I don't wan - na be a stu - pid girl. ___

Em
Am
Ba - by, if I act like that
flip - pin' my blond hair back.
Em
Am
Push up my bra like that.
I don't wan - na be a stu - pid girl.
Em
Am
Girls, stu - pid girls.
Stu - pid girls.
Em
Am
Repeat and Fade
Optional Ending
Em
Stu - pid girls.
Stu - pid girls.

WHO KNEW

Words and Music by ALECIA MOORE,
MAX MARTIN and LUKASZ GOTTWALD

* Vocal is written one octave higher than sung.

F♯m E

that's right.
no, no.

A

I took your words and I be - lieved
I wish I could touch you a - gain;

in ev - 'ry - thing you said to me,
I wish I could still call you friend.

Bm F♯m E

yah, huh, that's right.
I'd give an - y - thing.

D5
5fr
If some - one said
When some - one said
E5
F♯5
three years from now you'd be long
count your bless - ings now 'fore they're long
A5
5fr
D5
5fr
gone, I'd stand up and
gone, I guess I just
E5
F♯5
punch them out, 'cause they're all
did - n't know how. I was all

A5 (5fr) — D5 (5fr) — E5

__ wrong. __ I __ know bet - ter,
__ wrong, __ but they __ knew bet - ter.

F♯5 — A5 (5fr) — D5 (5fr)

'cause __ / Still, __ you said __ for - ev - er and ev - er.

E5 — A

Who __ knew? ____

1 — 2

Bm
F♯m
E
I'll keep you locked in my head until we meet again.
A
(Until we, until we meet again.)
Bm
And I won't forget you, my friend.
F♯m
E
What happened? If

D5 E5 F♯5

some - one said three years from now you'd be long

A5 D5 E5

gone, I'd stand up and punch them out,

F♯5 A5

'cause they're all wrong, and

D5 E5 F♯5

that last kiss I'll cher - ish un - til we meet

A5
5fr
D5
5fr
E5
again.
And time makes it hard - er.
F♯5
A5
5fr
D5
5fr
I wish I could re - mem - ber,
but I keep
E5
F♯5
A5
5fr
your mem - 'ry:
you vis - it me in my sleep.
D5
5fr
E5
A
My dar - ling,
who knew?

My dar - ling, my dar - ling, who _ knew?
My dar - ling, I miss _ you, my dar - ling.
Who _ knew?
Who _ knew?

U & UR HAND

Words and Music by ALECIA MOORE,
MAX MARTIN, LUKASZ GOTTWALD and RAMI

* Vocal line is written one octave higher than sung.

F5
D5
E5
to - night.
At the door we don't
Buh - bye.
Lis - ten up: it's
G5
D5
E5
G5
D5
E5
wait, 'cause we know them.
At the bar, six shots, just be - gin - ning.
just not hap - pen - ing.
You can say what you want to your boy - friends.
G5
D5
E5
F5
That's when dick - head put his hands on me,
but you see,
Just let me have my fun to - night,
ai - ight?
D5
E5
Em
Cmaj7
Cmaj13
I'm not here for your en - ter - tain - ment.

G
D5
5fr
D7(no3rd)
Em
You don't real - ly wan - na mess with me to - night. Just stop and
Cmaj7
Cmaj13
3fr
G
D
Dsus
D5
5fr
take a sec - ond. I was fine be - fore you walked in - to my life.
A7sus
G/C
Em
'Cause you know it's o - ver be - fore it
Em7/A
C
be - gan. Keep your drink; just give me the mon - ey;

G5
D
Dsus
D5
3fr
5fr
N.C.
it's just you and your hand to - night.
E5
G5
D5
E5
You're in the cor - ner with your boys. You bet them five bucks you'd get the girl that just walked
in, but she thinks you suck. We did - n't get all dressed up just for you to see,

G5
D5
E5
3fr
5fr
N.C.
so quit spill - ing your drinks on me, yeah.
(Spoken:) You know who you are,...high five-ing, talking shit, but you're going home alone, aren't ya?
'Cause
Em
Cmaj7
Cmaj13
3fr
G
I'm not here for your en - ter - tain - ment.
You don't real - ly wan - na
D5
5fr
D7(no3rd)
Em
Cmaj7
Cmaj13
3fr
mess with me to - night.
Just stop and take a sec - ond.

G D Dsus D5 A7sus

I was fine be-fore you walked in-to my life. 'Cause you know

G/C Em(add4)

it's o-ver be-fore it be-gan.

Em7/A C G5

Keep your drink; just give me the mon-ey; it's just you and your

D Dsus D5 N.C.

hand to-night. Hand, oh.

DEAR MR. PRESIDENT

Words and Music by ALECIA MOORE
and BILLY MANN

Gm11
F/A
Were you a lone - ly boy? (Are you a lone - ly boy?)
B♭sus2
Let's pre - tend we're just two peo - ple and
How can you say, "no child is left be - hind?"
F/A
Gm11
you're not bet - ter than me. I'd like to ask you some
We're not dumb and we're not blind. They're all sit - ting
F/A
ques-tions if we can speak hon - est - ly.
in your cells while you pave the road to hell.

E♭
B♭/D
Cm
What do you feel when you see all the home - less on the street?
What kind of fa - ther would take his own daugh - ter's rights a - way?
B♭
F/A
Who do you pray for at night be - fore you go to sleep?
And what kind of fa - ther might hate his own daugh - ter if she were gay?
To Coda
What do you feel

Cm
3fr
Gm
3fr
F(add4)
3fr
Fsus
when you look in the mir - ror?
Are you proud?
E♭sus2
6fr
E♭
3fr
B♭
How do you sleep while the rest
F
Cm
3fr
B♭/D
E♭
3fr
of us cry?
How do you dream
B♭
F
Cm
3fr
Dm
E♭
3fr
when a moth - er has no chance to say good-bye?

E♭
3fr
F
B♭
F
How do you walk with your head held high?
E♭
3fr
Gm
3fr
Can you e - ven look me
F/A
E♭(add2)
6fr
in the eye
and tell me why?
B♭sus2
F/A

Gm11
F/A
D.S. al Coda
CODA
E♭
3fr
B♭/D
I can on - ly i - mag -
Cm
3fr
B♭
- ine what the first la - dy has to say.
F/A
Gm
3fr
You've come a long way
from whis - key and co -

C7
C7sus
C
Csus
3fr
B♭
caine.
How do you sleep while the rest
F
Cm
3fr
B♭/D
E♭
3fr
of us cry?
How do you dream
B♭
F
Cm
3fr
Dm
E♭
3fr
when a moth - er has no chance to say good - bye?
B♭
F
How do you walk with your head held high?

E♭
3fr
Gm
3fr
Can you e - ven look me
F/A
E♭
3fr
in the eye?
Let me tell you 'bout hard
Gm
3fr
F/A
B♭
work,
min - i - mum wage
B♭/D
E♭
3fr
with a ba - by on the way.
Let me tell you 'bout hard

Gm
F/A
B♭
work, re - build - ing your house
Cm
B♭/D
E♭
after the bombs took them a - way. Let me tell you 'bout hard
Gm
F/A
B♭
Cm
B♭/D
work, build - ing a bed out of a card - board box.
E♭
Gm
F/A
B♭
Let me tell you 'bout hard work, hard work, hard

Cm
B♭/D
E♭
Gm
F/A
work.
You don't know noth - ing 'bout hard work, hard
B♭
Cm
B♭/D
E♭
work, hard work.
E♭sus2
B♭
F/A
How do you sleep at night?

Gm7
F/A
How do you walk with your
B♭
head held high? Dear Mis - ter Pres - i - dent,
F/A
you'd nev - er take a walk with me,
Gm11
F/A
hmmm, would you?
rit.

SO WHAT

Words and Music by ALECIA MOORE,
MAX MARTIN and JOHAN SCHUSTER

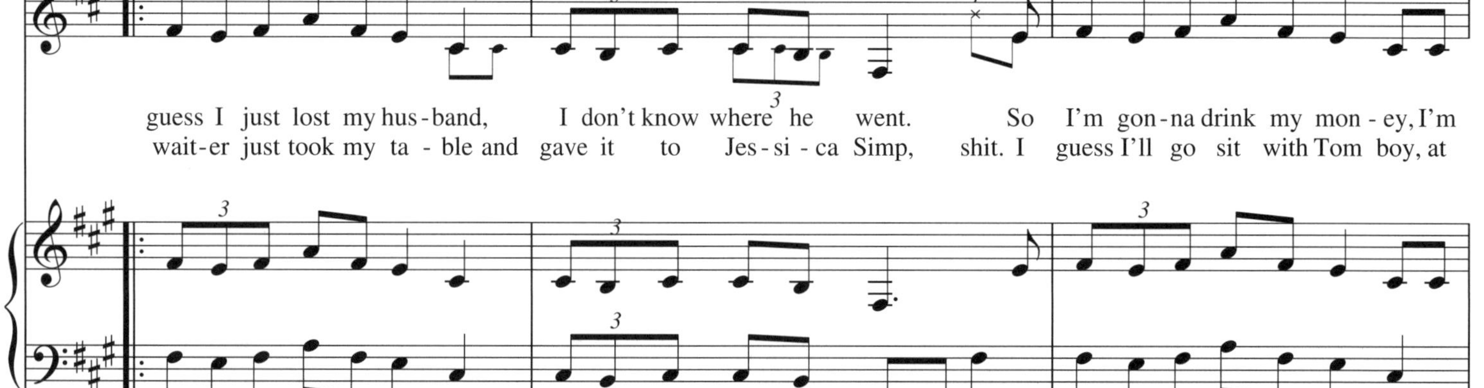

not gon - na pay his rent, nope. I got a brand - new at - ti - tude and I'm gon - na wear it to - night.
least he'll know how to hit. What if this song's on the ra - di - o, then some - bod - y's gon - na die.
I'm gon - na get in trou - ble, I wan - na start a fight. Na, na, na, na, na, na, na,
I'm gon - na get in trou - ble, my ex will start a fight. Na, na, na, na, na, na, na,
I wan - na start a fight. Na, na, na, na, na, na, na, I wan - na start a fight.
he's gon - na start a fight. Na, na, na, na, na, na, na, we're all gon - na get in a fight.
So,
A5
5fr
C♯5
4fr
F♯5
so what? I'm still a rock star. I got my rock moves and I don't

D5
A5
C♯5
need you. And guess what? I'm hav - in' more fun. And now that
F♯5
D5
A5
we're done, I'm gon - na show you to - night I'm al - right,
C♯5
F♯5
D5
I'm just fine, and you're a tool. So,
A5
C♯5
F♯5
To Coda
so what? I am a rock star. I got my rock moves and I don't

D5
5fr
1
N.C.
want you to - night. Uh, check my flow, uh. The
2
A5
5fr
A
You were - n't there,
you nev - er were. You want it all but that's not fair.
I gave you life, I gave my all. You were - n't there,

A5
5fr
D.S. al Coda
you let me fall.
So,
CODA
D5
5fr
A5
5fr
C♯5
4fr
want you to - night,
no, no.
No, no,
F♯5
D5
5fr
A5
5fr
I don't want you to - night.
C♯5
4fr
F♯5
D5
5fr
You were - n't there.
I'm gon - na show you to - night

A5
C♯5
F♯5
I'm al - right,
I'm just fine,
and you're a
D5
A5
C♯5
tool. So,
so what? I am a rock star. I got my
F♯5
D5
N.C.
rock moves and I don't want you to - night.
Ba, da, da, da, da, da, pfft.

SOBER

Words and Music by ALECIA MOORE,
KARA DioGUARDI, NATHANIEL HILLS
and MARCELLA ARAICA

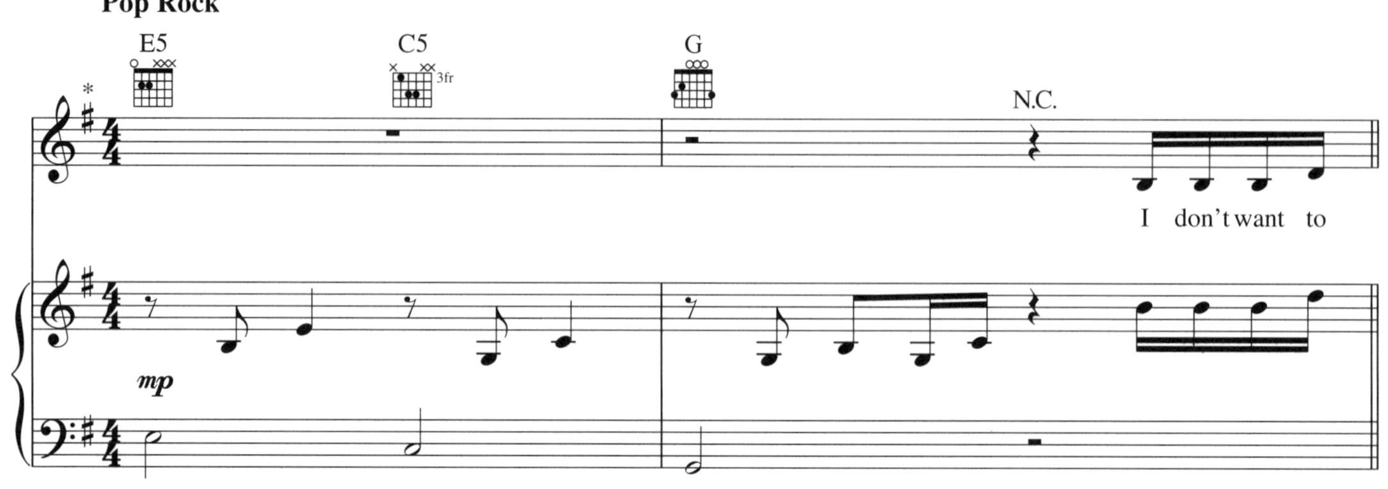

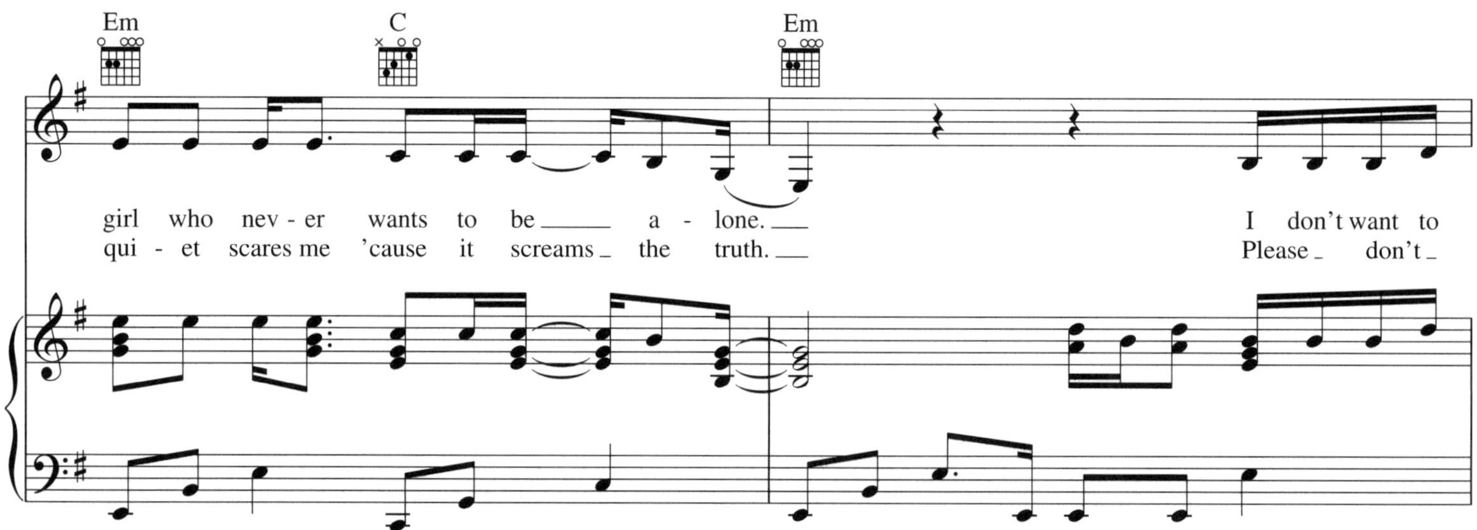

* *Recorded a half step lower.*

C
G
Gsus
3fr
G
be that call at four o' - clock _ in the morn - ing 'cause I'm the
tell me that we had that con - ver - sa - tion, _ 'cause I won't re -
Em
C
Em
on - ly one you know in the world that won't _ be home. _
mem - ber. _ Save your _ breath, 'cause what's _ the use? _
G
C
Em
Ah, _ the sun is blind - ing,
Ah, _ the night is call - ing, and it
G
Am
Em
I _ stayed up a - gain. _
whis - pers to me soft - ly, "Come and play." _

G
C
Em
Oh, I am find - ing
I, I am fall - ing and if I
G
Am
Em
that's not the way I want my sto - ry to end.
let my - self go, I'm the on - ly one to blame.
C
G
Am
I'm safe up high, noth - ing can touch me, but why do I feel this par - ty's o - ver?
Em
C
G
No pain in - side, you're my pro - tec - tion, but

Am
1
Em
how do I feel this good so - ber?
I don't want to
2
Em
C
Com - ing down, com - ing down, com - ing down, spin - ning
G
Am
round, spin - ning round, spin - ning round, I'm look - ing for my - self so -
Em
C
ber. Com - ing down, com - ing down, com - ing down, spin - ning

G Am

round, spin-ning round, spin-ning round, ___ look-ing for my-self so-

Em C

ber. ___ When it's good, then it's good, it's so ___ good 'til it goes ___

G Em

___ bad, 'til you're try-ing to find ___ the you ___ that you ___ once had. ___

D C

___ I have heard my-self cry, ___ "Nev-er a-gain," ___

G
G/D
D
broken down in agony and just
trying to find a friend.
Em
Cmaj7
Oh,
G
Em
Cmaj7
Em
oh.
C
G
Am
I'm safe up high, nothing can touch me, but why do I feel this party's over?

Em
C
G
No pain in - side, you're my pro-tec - tion, but
Am
1
Em
2
Em
how do I feel this good sober?
3
3
C
G
Am
Em
C
G
Am
E5

PLEASE DON'T LEAVE ME

Words and Music by ALECIA MOORE
and MAX MARTIN

Upbeat Pop-Rock

** Recorded a half step lower.*

D

I don't know if I could yell an - y loud - er.
How did I be - come___ so ob - nox - ious?

A

How man - y times have I kicked you out of here
What is it with you that makes me act like this?

Bm

or said some - thing___ in - sult - ing?
I've nev - er been___ this nas - ty.

G

(Da da da___ da da.)
(Da da da___ da da.)

D
I can be so mean ___ when I want to be,
Can't you tell that this is all just a con - test?
A
I am ca - pa - ble ___ of real - ly an - y - thing.
The one that wins will be the one that hits the hard - est.
Bm
I can cut you in - to piec - es
But, ba - by, I ___ don't mean ___ it.
G
when my heart ___ is bro -
I mean ___ it, I

A
D
- ken.
promise.
(Da da da da da.)
(Da da da da da.)
Please
A
Bm
G
don't leave me.
D
A
Bm
Please
don't leave me.
G
D
A
I always say how I don't need you, but it's

Bm
G
Bm
always gonna come right back to this. Please
1
A/C♯
D
G
don't leave me. (Da da da da da.)
2
A/C♯
D
don't leave me. I for-
A
Bm
D
got to say out loud how beau-ti-ful you real-ly

A
are to me. I can't be with - out; you're my
Bm
D
G
per - fect lit - tle punch - ing bag, and I need you.
Asus
I'm sor - ry. (Da da da da da.)
D
A
Bm
Da da da da, da da da da.

G
D
A
Da da da da da. Please, please don't leave
Bm
G
D
me. Ba - by... Please
A
Bm
G
don't leave me.
D
A
Bm
Please don't leave me.

G
D
A
I al - ways say how I don't need you, but it's
Bm
G
Bm
al - ways gon - na come right back to this.
A/C♯
D
G
Please don't leave me. Ba - by,
Bm
A/C♯
D
please, please don't leave me.

GLITTER IN THE AIR

Words and Music by ALECIA MOORE
and BILLY MANN

Gm7 F/A B♭ Gm7 F/A B♭
Have you ev - er thrown a hand - ful of glit - ter in the
Have you ev - er been touched so gen - tly you had to
F5 F5/E Dm7 F5/C Dm7 F5/C F5/B♭ F/A
3fr
air? Have you
cry?
Gm7 F/A B♭ Gm7 F/A B♭
ev - er looked fear in the face and said, "I just don't
Have you ev - er in - vit - ed a stran - ger to come in -
F5 F5/E Dm7 F5/C Dm7 F5/C F5/B♭ F/A C
care?" It's on - ly half past the
side? It's on - ly half past the

B♭
C
point of no re - turn, the tip of the ice - berg, the
point of o - bliv - i - on, the ho - ur - glass on the ta - ble, the
B♭
F
sun be - fore the burn. The thun - der be - fore the light - ning, and the
walk be - fore the run. The breath be - fore the kiss, and the
C
B♭
breath be - fore the phrase. Have you ev - er felt this way?
fear be - fore the phrase. Have you ev - er felt this way?
F5
F5/E
Dm7
F5/C
Dm7
F5/C
F5/B♭
F/A
1
F5
F5/E
Dm7
F5/C
3fr

Dm7
F5/C
F5/B♭
F/A
2
F5
F5/E
B♭/D
F/C
B♭/D
Am/C
Gm/B♭
F/A
3fr
La la la la la la la la.
F5
C/E
B♭/D
F/C
B♭/D
C
Gm/B♭
F/A
Dm
There you were
G
Dm
G
sit - ting in the gar - den, clutch - ing my cof - fee, call - ing me
F
C/E
Dm
sug - ar, you called me sug - ar.

C/E
F
C/E
Oh,
no, no, no,
Dm
C/E
F5
F5/E
Dm7
F5/C
3fr
no.
Have you ev - er
Dm7
F5/C
F5/B♭
F/A
F5
F5/E
Dm7
F5/C
Dm7
F5/C
F5/B♭
F/A
wished for an end - less night?
F5
F5/E
Dm7
F5/C
Dm7
F5/C
F5/B♭
F/A
Las - soed the moon and the stars and pulled that

F5
F5/E
Dm7
F5/C
Dm7
F5/C
F5/B♭
F/A
Gm7
F/A
B♭
N.C.
rope tight?
Have you ev-er
held your breath and asked your - self will it
ev - er get bet - ter than to - night?
To - night.
F

RAISE YOUR GLASS

Words and Music by ALECIA MOORE,
MAX MARTIN and JOHAN SCHUSTER

G D C
I love when it's all too much. Five a. m., turn the ra - di - o up.
Can't stop, com - in' in hot. I should be locked up right on the spot.
Em D
Where's the rock and roll?
It's so on right now. *It's so fuckin' on right now.*
G D C
Par - ty - crash - er, pen - ny - snatch - er,
Em D
call me up if you a gang - sta.

G
D
C
Csus2
3fr
Don't be fan - cy; just get danc - y.
Why so se - ri - ous?
G
D
C
So raise your glass if you are wrong
Em
D
in all the right ways, all my un - der - dogs.
G
D
C
We will nev - er be, nev - er be an - y - thing but loud

Em
D
and nit - ty - grit - ty, dirt - y lit - tle freaks.
G
D
C
Won't you come on and, come on and raise your glass?
Em
D
Just come on and, come on and raise your glass.
1
2, 3
Won't you come on and, come on and

To Coda
G
D
C
raise your glass? / glass
Just come on and, come on and
Em
D
raise your glass.
G
D
C
Oh, shit! My glass is empty.
That sucks!
Em
D
So if you're
G
D
C
too school_ for cool___
and you're treat - ed like__ a fool,__

Em D G D C
you can choose to let it go. We can al - ways,
Csus2
we can al - ways par - ty on our own. So raise your...
G D C
... aw, fuck! So raise your glass if you are wrong
Em D
in all the right ways, all my un - der - dogs.

G
D
C
We will nev-er be, nev-er be an - y - thing but loud
Em
D
and nit - ty - grit - ty, dirt - y lit - tle freaks.
D.S. al Coda
(take 2nd ending)
So raise your
CODA
for me? Just come on and, come on and
Em
D
G5
3fr
raise your glass for me.

F***IN' PERFECT

Words and Music by ALECIA MOORE,
MAX MARTIN and JOHAN SCHUSTER

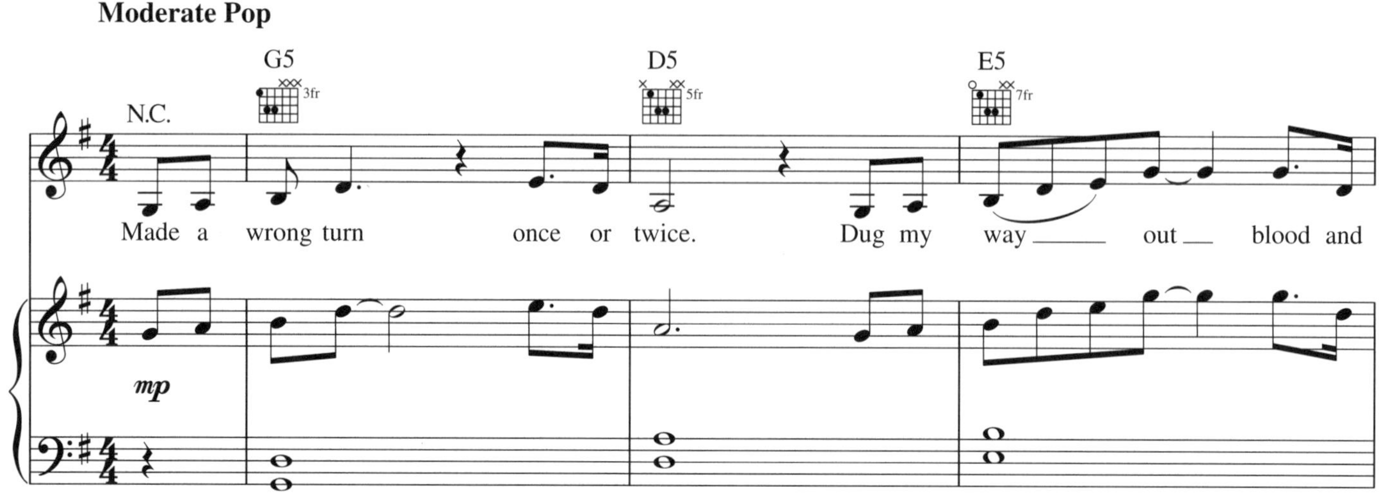

Dsus
Em
Csus2
stood. Miss know it, it's all good. It did - n't slow me down. Mis -
make it. Filled with so much hat - red, such a tired game. It's e -
G5
Dsus
Em
tak - en. Al - ways sec - ond guess - ing, un - der - es - ti - mat - ing. Look, I'm still a -
nough, I've done all I can think of. Chased down all my de - mons, I've seen you do the
Csus2
G5
Dsus
round.
same.
Pret - ty, pret - ty please don't you ev - er, ev - er feel like you're
Em
Csus2
G5
less than fuck - in' per - fect. Pret - ty, pret - ty please, if you

Dsus
Em
Csus2
To Coda
3fr
ev - er, ev - er feel like you're noth - in', you're fuck - in' per - fect to me.
G5
3fr
Dsus
You're so mean when you talk a - bout your -
Em
Csus2
3fr
G5
3fr
self. You were wrong. Change the voic - es in your
Dsus
Em
Csus2
3fr
D.S. al Coda
head, make them like you in - stead. So com - pli -

CODA
Csus2
G5
per - fect to me.
The whole world's scared so I swal - low the fear. The on - ly
D
Em
thing I should be drink - in' is an ice cold beer. So cool in line and we try, try, try but we
C
G5
try so hard and it's a waste of my time. Done look - in' for the crit - ics 'cause they're ev - 'ry - where. They don't
D
Em
like my jeans, they don't get my hair. Ex - change our - selves and we do it all the time.

C
G5
Why do we do __ that? Why do I do __ that? (Spoken:) Why do I do that? Yeah. ______
Dsus
Em
Csus2
3fr
G5
Dsus
Em
Pret-ty, pret-ty please don't you ev-er, ev-er feel like you're less than __ fuck-in'
Csus2
G5
Dsus
per - fect. __ Pret-ty, pret-ty please if you ev-er, ev-er feel like you're

Em
Csus2
3fr
G5
3fr
noth - in', you're fuck - in' per - fect to me.
Dsus
Em
Csus2
3fr
G5
3fr
Dsus
Pret - ty, pret - ty please if you ev - er, ev - er feel like you're
Em
Csus2
3fr
G5
3fr
noth - in', you're fuck - in' per - fect to me.